THE BLACK WIDOW SPIDER

BY LISA OWINGS

BELLWETHER MEDIA · MINNEAPOLIS, MN

Jump into the cockpit and take flight with Pilot books. Your journey will take you on high-energy adventures as you learn about all that is wild, weird, fascinating, and fun!

This edition first published in 2013 by Bellwether Media, Inc.

No part of this publication may be reproduced in whole or in part without written permission of the publisher.
For information regarding permission, write to Bellwether Media, Inc., Attention: Permissions Department,
5357 Penn Avenue South, Minneapolis, MN 55419.

Library of Congress Cataloging-in-Publication Data

Owings, Lisa.
  The black widow spider / by Lisa Owings.
    pages cm. – (Pilot. Nature's deadliest)
  Audience: 8-12
  Includes bibliographical references and index.
  Summary: "Fascinating images accompany information about the black widow spider. The combination of high-interest
subject matter and narrative text is intended for students in grades 3 through 7"– Provided by publisher.
  ISBN 978-1-60014-878-1 (hardcover : alk. paper)
  1. Black widow spider–Juvenile literature. I. Title.
  QL458.42.T54O95 2013
  595.4'4-dc23
                              2012034292

Printed in the United States of America, North Mankato, MN.

CONTENTS

Breakfast

"Mikey, come eat!" Fifteen-year-old Mike Makens heard his mom calling him to breakfast. He grabbed a pair of socks and rushed to put them on. As he slid one foot in, he felt a sharp prick. It wasn't too painful. It was probably nothing to worry about. Mike shrugged it off and joined his family at the table in their Colorado home.

After breakfast, Mike felt another prick. This time he was sure there was something in his sock. He pulled it

Fair-Weather Frights

Black widow spiders prefer warm weather. However, that doesn't stop them from living in cooler climates. They move indoors when it starts to get chilly.

Mike brushed the dead spider onto the counter to take a closer look. Its body was glossy black. Suddenly, Mike's gut twisted in fear. He noticed a familiar marking on the spider's **abdomen**. There was no mistaking it. It was the red **hourglass** of the black **widow**. Mike had been bitten by one of the deadliest spiders on Earth.

Within minutes, Mike was in such extreme pain that he collapsed to the floor. It felt like his entire leg was being stabbed with knives. The pain grew worse and worse. Mike's screams and sobs were too much for his parents to bear. They rushed him to the nearest hospital.

Doctors gave Mike medicine for the pain. Unfortunately, it didn't give him the relief he so desperately needed. Black widow **antivenom** was the only thing that could bring an end to his **torture**. There was one kind available in the United States, but its **side effects** could kill him. Mike's family had heard about a safer kind of antivenom. However, finding it would be difficult.

Black Widow Antivenom

In the United States, horses are injected with small amounts of black widow venom. Their bodies react by producing a substance that stops the effects of the venom. Doctors use this substance to make antivenom.

Mike's parents decided it was worth a try. It took a week to get the antivenom from Mexico. Each day without it was **agony** for Mike. Then the hospital refused to treat him with it. The people in charge were afraid it might be illegal. Luckily, Mike's doctor agreed to give Mike the antivenom outside the hospital. It worked almost immediately. Mike went home less than two hours later.

The Lethal Lady

Several **species** of spiders are called black widows. These spiders are found around the world in **temperate** climates. Female black widows are the true killers. Their shiny black bodies are around 1 inch (2.5 centimeters) long. That makes them about two to four times the size of males. On the underside of a female's round abdomen is a blood-red hourglass. Some females have orange or yellow hourglass markings.

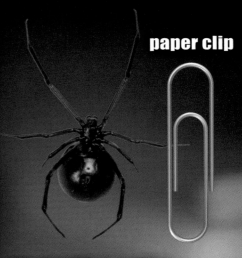

paper clip

black widow spider

N
W — E
S

black widow territory =

false widow spider

Poisonous Pretenders

False widow spiders are often mistaken for black widows. They have a similar body shape but no hourglass markings. False widow bites are less dangerous than black widow bites.

The black widow spider has a creepy name and a deadly **reputation**. The female black widow is responsible for both. The name comes from her habit of eating her male partner after mating. The reputation comes from her powerful **venom**. It can be **lethal** for children and unhealthy adults.

Blind as a Black Widow
The black widow has eight eyes but poor vision. She "sees" by feeling vibrations in her web.

The black widow's web isn't beautiful, but it is home. She waits there until an unlucky insect gets caught in the sticky strands. The black widow uses her hairy legs to wrap the threads around her prey. Then she delivers a deadly bite. Venom flows through her **fangs** and **paralyzes** her prey. Other chemicals turn the victim's insides into liquid. The black widow sucks up her meal. Then she cuts the skeleton loose.

A black widow bite can also spell death for humans. The venom causes severe pain and cramping as it spreads throughout the body. It can also cause **nausea** and make breathing difficult. Symptoms often last for several days. The agony of the black widow's bite is the last thing some of her victims will ever feel.

Other Black Widow Bite Symptoms:

- increased heart rate
- dizziness
- fainting
- chills
- fever
- sweating
- shaking
- weakness
- headache

female

male

14

A female black widow lives alone. She allows a male onto her web only during mating season. The male approaches cautiously. He dances gently on her web. If she likes his dance, she will mate with him. However, she may decide afterward to wrap him in silk and slurp up his insides.

The female lays several egg sacs in the months after mating. Each papery sac contains hundreds of eggs. An army of young black widow spiders hatches within a few weeks. Many die or are eaten by their siblings shortly after hatching. Soon the survivors are ready to leave the web. They climb to a high place. Then they cast their silk into the wind and **balloon** to their new home.

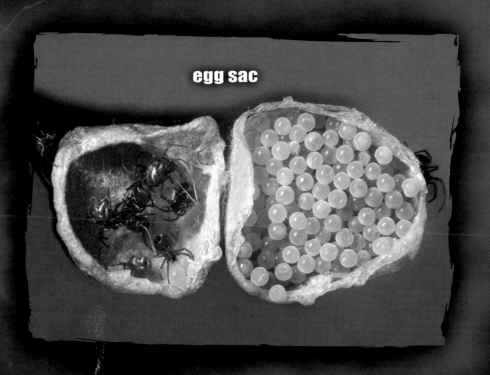

egg sac

Black Widow Attacks

Black widows usually do not attack people unless they feel threatened and cannot get away. They are more likely to bite when protecting their eggs. People are often bitten after accidentally disturbing a black widow's web.

You can prevent a black widow attack by being careful in black widow habitats. These spiders prefer dark, sheltered places. Wear gloves, shoes, and long clothing anywhere they might be hiding. Black widows often crawl into dressers and closets. Shake out rarely worn clothes and shoes before putting them on. Always look out for the messy web of a black widow. To be safe, keep your distance from any spider you spot.

Take Action

It is best to relocate a black widow found in or near your home. Use gloves and a broom or shovel to move the spider. Call pest control if you find

not feel it. However, the painful symptoms that follow are easy to recognize. They usually begin within an hour. Get to a hospital right away if you think you have been bitten by a black widow. Call ahead if you are having a severe reaction so doctors will be ready to treat you.

While waiting to be treated, wash the bite with soap and water. Tie a bandage firmly above the bite if it is on an arm or leg. Keep the limb still and raised above your heart if possible. This slows the spread of venom. An ice pack or cold cloth helps keep the area around the bite from swelling. At the hospital, doctors may give you strong pain medication or black widow antivenom.

Gotcha!

If you can, put on gloves and trap the spider that bit you. Place it in a container and bring it with you to the hospital. This will help doctors know exactly how to treat you.

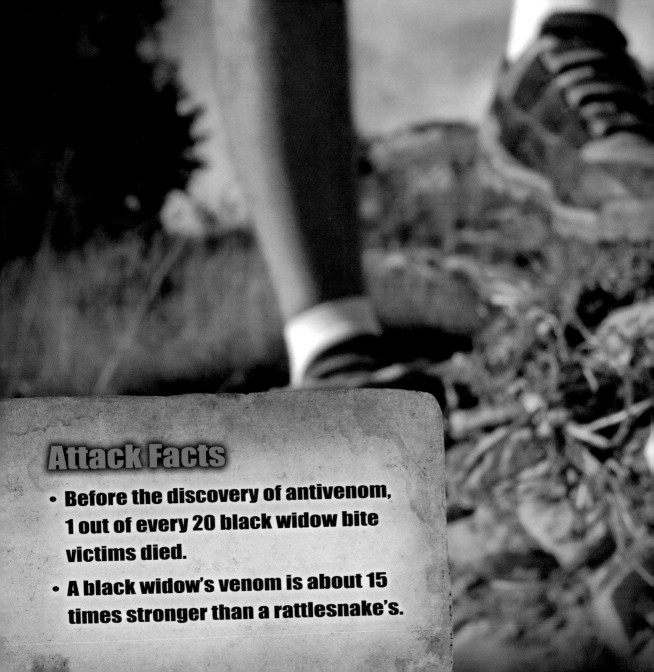

Attack Facts

- Before the discovery of antivenom, 1 out of every 20 black widow bite victims died.

- A black widow's venom is about 15 times stronger than a rattlesnake's.

Many black widow species live near people. However, most people have no idea if they are sharing their home with a black widow. This is because black widows are shy. They avoid human activity and bite only when bothered.

Learning about black widows is important because the spiders are both common and deadly. Find out which black widow species live near you. Make sure you can easily identify them. If you catch sight of a red hourglass, it's time to get away!

abdomen—the rear section of a spider's body

agony—severe pain

antivenom—a substance that acts against venom and treats the effects of a venomous bite

balloon—to travel through the air like a floating balloon; baby spiders travel this way by letting a strand of their silk catch the wind.

fangs—the pointed teeth of spiders and some other venomous animals; fangs are hollow or grooved to guide venom into prey.

hourglass—a device used for measuring time; an hourglass shape looks like a rectangle with its long sides pinched together.

lethal—deadly

nausea—a feeling of wanting to throw up

paralyzes—causes the loss of movement or feeling

reputation—the way someone or something is generally viewed

side effects—negative effects of a medicine

species—a type of animal or plant

temperate—neither too warm nor too cold

torture—extreme pain or suffering

venom—poison produced by some animals to kill or paralyze prey

widow—a woman whose husband has died

To Learn More

At the Library

Markle, Sandra. *Black Widows: Deadly Biters*. Minneapolis, Minn.: Lerner Publications, 2011.

McFee, Shane. *Deadly Spiders*. New York, N.Y.: PowerKids Press, 2008.

Roza, Greg. *Deadly Black Widows*. New York, N.Y.: Gareth Stevens Pub., 2012.

On the Web

Learning more about black widow spiders is as easy as 1, 2, 3.

1. Go to www.factsurfer.com.

2. Enter "black widow spiders" into the search box.

3. Click the "Surf" button and you will see a list of related Web sites.

With factsurfer.com, finding more information is just a click away.

Index